Science Alive

Light and Dark

Terry Jennings

FRANKLIN WATTS
LONDON•SYDNEY

Appleseed Editions Ltd
Well House, Friars Hill, Guestling, East Sussex TN35 4ET

Created by Q2A Media
Series Editor: Honor Head
Book Editor: Katie Dicker
Senior Art Designers: Ashita Murgai, Nishant Mudgal
Designers: Diksha Khatri, Harleen Mehta
Picture Researcher: Poloumi Ghosh
Line Artists: Indernil Ganguly, Rishi Bhardhwaj
Illustrators: Kusum Kala, Manish Prasad, Sanyogita Lal

ISBN   978 0 7496 7559 2

Dewey classification: 535

All words in **bold** can be found in 'Words to remember' on pages 30-31.

Website information is correct at time of going to press. However, the publishers cannot
accept liability for any information or links found on third-party websites.

A CIP catalogue for this book is available from the British Library.

Picture credits
t=top b=bottom c=centre l=left r=right m=middle
Cover Images: Main Image: David Young-Wolff / Alamy; Small Image: WizData, inc. / Shutterstock
Index Stock Imagery/ Photolibrary: 4r, mk/ Shutterstock: 6m, Yanik Chauvin/ Shutterstock: 10,
Chuck Savage/ Corbis: 11m, pending:13t, JLP/ Jose Luis Pelaez/zefa/ Corbis: 13b, Ariel Skelley/ Corbis: 16l, Romilly
Lockyer/ Gettyimages: 17, Trevor Bauer/ Istockphoto: 20b, Roger Ressmeyer/ Corbis: 21r, Moritz von Hacht/
Istockphoto: 25t, David Godwin: 25b, Index Stock Imagery/ Photolibrary: 26b, Chee-Onn Leong/ Shutterstock: 27b,
Otmar Smit/ Shutterstock: 28b.

Printed in China

Franklin Watts is a division of Hachette Children's Books

Contents

Sunlight

Our world is full of light. During the day, most of our light comes from the sun. At the end of the day it gets dark because the sun goes down.

▶ At night, it is dark because there isn't any sunlight. A torch can help to turn some of the darkness into light.

Making shadows

During the day, if you stand with your back to the sun, you may see a dark shape on the ground in front of you. This is called a **shadow**. Shadows form because light travels in straight lines. Light cannot go around things.

▲ *When the sun shines, a dark shadow of this boy appears on the ground. The sunlight cannot travel through the boy's body. The kite is made from paper. Some sunlight passes through the kite, so this shadow is not as dark.*

How light travels

Light travels in straight lines – it cannot bend. However, there are times when light looks as if it is bending.

▲ *In this forest, you can see rays of light travelling in straight lines. The bright sunlight is shining on the mist in the air.*

Changing speed

Light travels faster through air than through water. When light changes speed it also changes direction – this is why objects look broken or bent when they are placed in water.

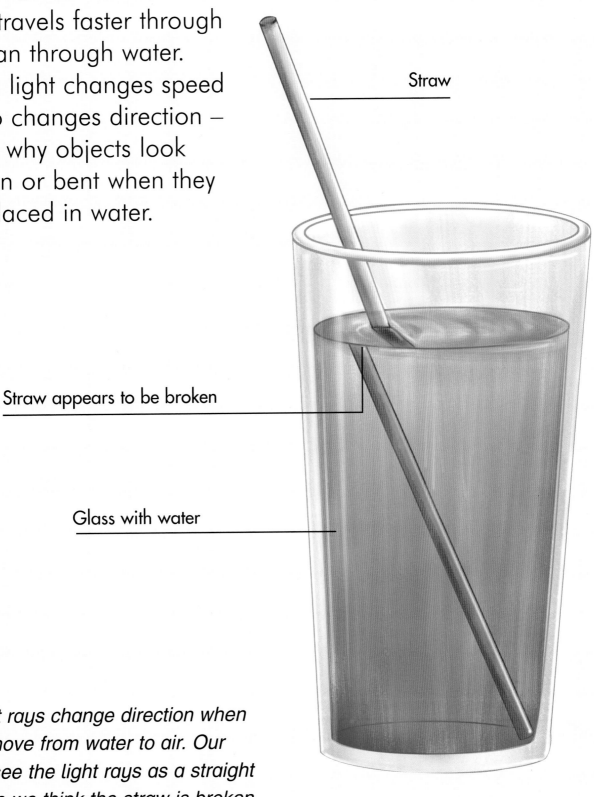

Straw

Straw appears to be broken

Glass with water

▶ *Light rays change direction when they move from water to air. Our eyes see the light rays as a straight line, so we think the straw is broken.*

Try this...

Magic cup

Find out how moving light rays change the objects that we see.

You will need
- a coin • a cup • a jug of water

1 Put the coin in the bottom of the cup.

2 Move away from the cup, so the coin is just out of view.

3 Slowly fill the cup with water from the jug. What can you see?

What happened?

When the coin is out of view, the sides of the cup stop the light rays from travelling from the coin to your eyes. When you fill the cup with water, the coin magically comes into view. Light rays from the coin change direction at the water's surface. The light rays can now reach your eyes and you see the coin again.

Lenses

We use **lenses** to make objects look bigger, smaller or even nearer. Lenses do this because they cause light rays to change direction.

◀ The lens in this magnifying glass makes the girl's eye look bigger.

Types of lenses

Lenses are usually made from glass or plastic. **Spectacles** are made with **convex lenses** or **concave lenses**. These lenses sharpen an image by making objects look bigger or smaller than they really are.

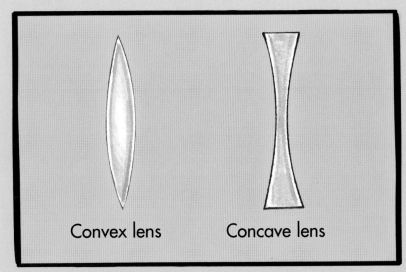

Convex lens   Concave lens

▲ *Convex lenses are wider in the middle than at the edges. Concave lenses are thinner in the middle than at the edges.*

▲ *People who are short-sighted wear glasses with concave lenses to help them see things in the distance. People who are long-sighted wear glasses with convex lenses to help them see close objects.*

Lenses at work

Lenses help us to find out more about the world around us. **Telescopes** and **microscopes** are instruments that use lenses.

Telescopes

A simple telescope is a long tube with a lens at each end. Telescopes make faraway objects seem much nearer.

▼ *Telescopes are useful for looking at objects in the distance.*

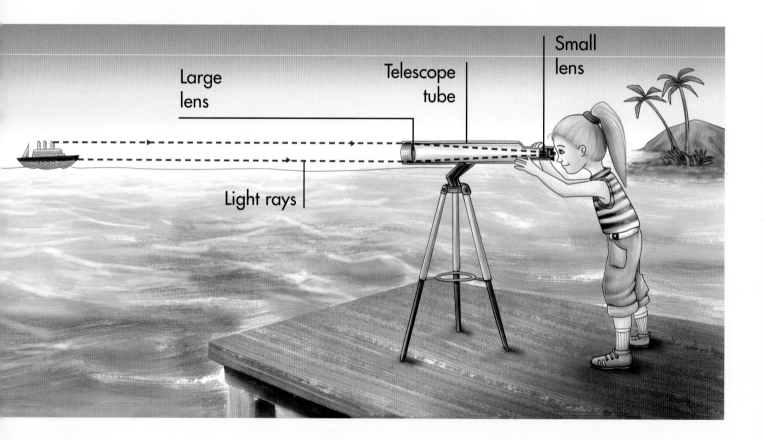

Large lens

Telescope tube

Small lens

Light rays

Microscopes

A microscope uses several lenses. It makes a small object look hundreds or thousands of times bigger than it really is.

▼ You can see the tiny veins in a leaf with a microscope.

▶ With a powerful microscope like this, you can magnify objects to look at them in more detail.

Try this...

Water droplet microscope

Discover how water can change the things that we see.

You will need
- a magazine • a sheet of cling film
- water

1. Place the magazine on a flat firm surface, such as a table. Cover the magazine with a sheet of cling film.

2. Put a drop of water on to the cling film. An eye-dropper is useful for this but you can also use a pencil or your little finger – dip them into the water and let a drop fall on to the cling film.

3 What effect does the drop of water have on the illustrations in the magazine?

What happened?

The drop of water acts like a convex lens. The water magnifies the light that reflects off the paper because it causes the light rays to change direction. This makes the illustration under the water drop look bigger.

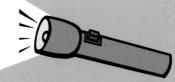

Bouncing light

We can see our **reflection** in a **mirror**. This is because light bounces off smooth, shiny surfaces made of glass or metal.

Mirrors

Most mirrors are made of polished glass. Light rays hit this smooth surface and bounce off at the same angle, to give a reflection. When light rays hit rough surfaces they bounce off in different directions so they do not give a reflection.

◀ *When light hits the surface of a mirror, nearly all the light bounces back into our eyes and we see a reflection.*

Different shaped mirrors

Not all mirrors are flat. A **convex mirror** curves outwards and makes objects looks smaller. A **concave mirror** curves inwards and makes objects look bigger.

◀ *Fairground mirrors are made from convex and concave mirrors. They make people look all sorts of funny shapes and sizes.*

Try this...

Light comb

This will show you how light reflects from a mirror.

You will need
- a sheet of cardboard • scissors • a comb • sticky tape
- a sheet of dark paper • modelling clay • a torch • a mirror

1 Ask an adult to cut a comb-shape along one edge of the cardboard, a little smaller than the actual comb.

2 Stick the comb to the cardboard so that it covers the hole. Put the sheet of dark paper on a table and use lumps of modelling clay to stand the card up at one end of the sheet of paper.

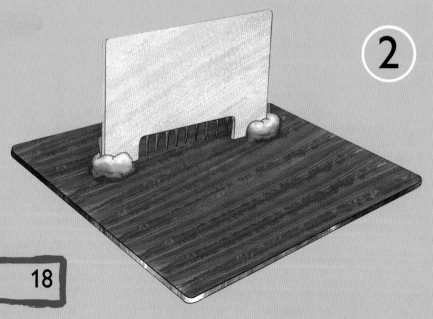

3 Shine a torch through the comb onto the dark paper. Hold a mirror in the path of the rays so that they bounce off it. What can you see?

What happened?

When the light shines through the comb, you can see light rays travelling in straight lines. The light rays are reflected and bounce off the mirror. If you turn the mirror, you can see that the reflections turn as well. The light rays are reflected at the same angle as they hit the mirror.

Colours

Everything around us has a colour. This is because light is made up of lots of different colours.

Sunlight

Sunlight looks white but it is really a mixture of many different colours. These colours can be seen when a **rainbow** forms.

▼ *When sunlight shines through rain, the different colours in the light change direction and spread out to form a rainbow.*

3 Hold the end of the pencil and stand it upright on a table. Spin the pencil fast. What can you see?

What happened?

When the wheel spins, all of the colours mix together and the wheel looks white. This is like the sunlight that we see. When a rainbow forms, the sunlight splits into its different colours, just like the colours of the wheel.

Light in nature

Most of our light comes from the sun. However, there are other forms of natural light. Some animals even make their own light.

Sun

Light rays

Earth

◀ *The sun is a huge ball of burning gases in space. Heat and light rays from the sun travel through space to reach our Earth.*

Lightning

During a storm, flashes of **lightning** can be seen. These are sparks of **electricity**. They are even brighter than the sun, but they only last for a fraction of a second.

◀ *Flashes of lightning brighten the sky during a storm. The sparks of electricity jump from cloud to cloud or from the clouds to the ground.*

Living lights

Some animals make their own light using chemicals inside their bodies. This is because they come out at night, or live in the dark parts of the ocean.

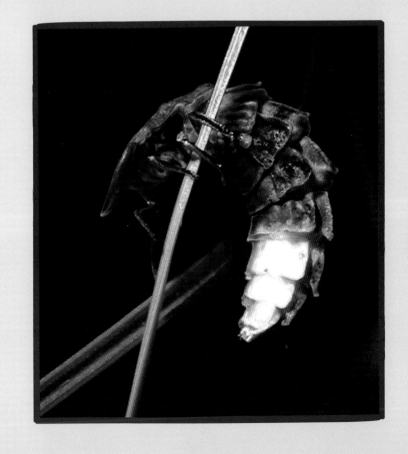

▶ *Glow-worms give out flashes of light in the dark to attract other glow-worms.*

Making light

We can make light in lots of different ways. However, most of the light that we make comes from electricity or fire.

Fire

When something burns it gives out light as well as heat. Before electric lights were invented, people used fires, flaming torches or oil lamps to help them to see at night.

◀ *Fire helps to light up the dark and can be seen for miles around. Fire can also be used to cook food and to keep people warm. But fire is dangerous and we must use it with care!*

Electric lights

At the touch of a switch we can turn electric light bulbs on or off. Inside a light bulb is a thin wire called a **filament**. This glows when the light is switched on. A light bulb is safer to use than a fire, because there is no flame that might burn us.

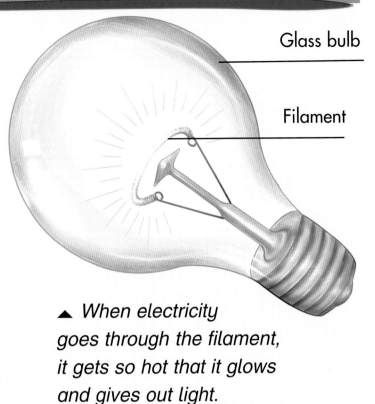

Glass bulb

Filament

▲ *When electricity goes through the filament, it gets so hot that it glows and gives out light.*

▲ *Electricity helps us to see at night. This city is lit up by the glow of thousands of light bulbs.*

Using light

Light has many other uses, too. Light can be used to make electricity. The speed at which light travels also helps us to send messages around the world.

Solar cells

Some watches and calculators are powered by sunlight. They have a **solar cell** on them that turns sunlight into electricity.

▼ *The **solar panels** on this roof use solar cells to turn sunlight into energy for the home.*

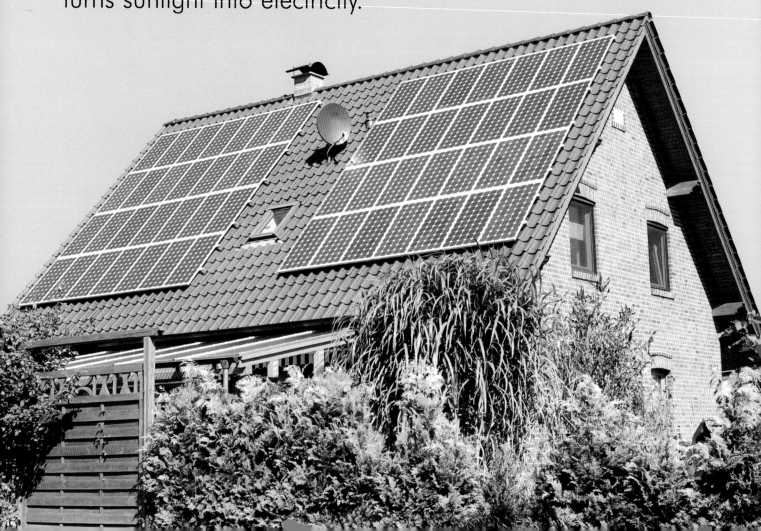

Carrying messages

Light travels at 300,000 kilometres per second. This is like travelling around the world seven times in a second! When we make telephone calls or send emails, the information is stored as rays of light and travels along wires filled with very tiny **fibres** of glass or plastic.

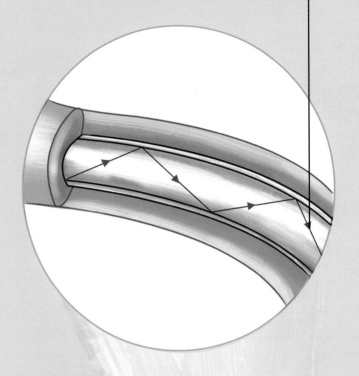

Light rays storing information travel quickly through each fibre

This wire contains lots of tiny fibres

Words to remember

Concave lenses
Lenses that are thinner in the middle than at the edges.

Concave mirror
A mirror that curves inwards.

Convex lenses
Lenses that are wider in the middle than at the edges.

Convex mirror
A mirror that curves outwards.

Electricity
A type of energy we can use to make things work.

Fibres
Very thin strands of material.

Filament
A thin wire inside a light bulb that glows when electricity runs through it.

Lenses
Pieces of glass or plastic with two curved surfaces.

Lightning
A flash of light caused when an electrical spark jumps between clouds or between a cloud and the ground.

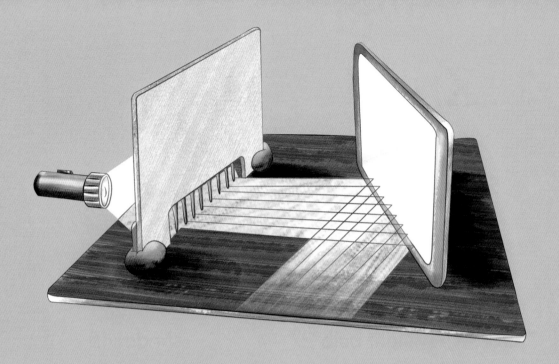

Microscopes
Devices that make small objects look bigger.

Mirror
A sheet of glass or metal that reflects an image.

Rainbow
The colours that form when sunlight passes through rain.

Reflection
The image seen in a mirror or other smooth, shiny surfaces.

Shadow
An area of darkness caused by an object blocking the light.

Solar cell
A device used to change light into electricity.

Solar panel
A group of solar cells.

Spectacles
A pair of lenses worn in front of the eyes to correct poor eyesight.

Telescopes
Devices that make distant objects look nearer.